This book belongs to

_ _ _ _ _ _ _ _ _ _ _ _

Hi, I'm Integrity Ninja. Today, I want to share a story with you about how I developed integrity. It all started one afternoon at practice...

It was my third and last try to score from the three-point line. I aimed, crouched a little, and threw the ball. It bounced off the backboard, rolled around the rim, and then fell off the wrong way.

"I wasn't watching. Was that a score?" Coach asked.
I didn't even think. "Yes, Coach!" I said.

Later, our art teacher said we could borrow one of her books if we were careful with them. I promised I would and took my favorite book filled with pictures of beautiful paintings. Oh, how I wished I could paint like that.

Our homework was to create a picture of a landscape. It could be any landscape at all, but the teacher wanted us to draw it from our imaginations.

At home, I paged through the book carefully. *This one!* I thought, happily, finding a picture of a wide landscape with a volcano puffing away in the middle. A village lay to one side, and the sea could be seen behind the volcano.

I tried to copy the painting by sketching it, but it kept going wrong. My volcano looked silly, and the village looked as though the buildings were wobbly.

Then, I had an idea. I took a sheet of paper and placed it over the picture.

Pressing firmly, I traced the whole picture - the volcano, the wide landscape, and the small village.

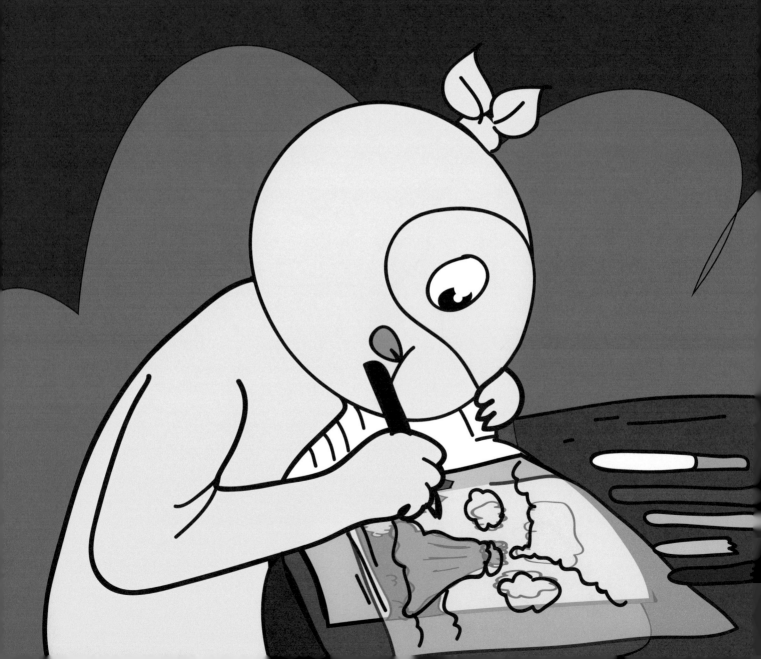

At last! I had a good landscape to color and set to work.

Just as I was finishing, Humble Ninja came over.

I picked up the teacher's book and showed Humble Ninja the picture.
She looked sad.

I turned a bright red. I didn't think anyone had seen it. Humble Ninja held the book up, turning the page.

I had pressed so hard with my pencil that the page underneath was marked with deep marks.

The next day, I brought my new drawing to class. It wasn't very good, but it was exciting. It was set in space, on an orange planet with three moons and two suns.

The ninjas all had flippers instead of feet, and they lived underwater.

I also brought back the damaged book.

I showed it to the teacher and promised her that I was going to replace it that weekend. I would use some of my savings to make it right. Teacher agreed that would be all right.

Then, at recess, I went to find Coach.

I felt relieved. No more bad secrets. And I liked that.

Keeping your promises and being honest could be your secret weapons in building your superpower of integrity!

Check out the Integrity Ninja lesson plans that contain fun activities to support the social, emotional lesson in this story at ninjalifehacks.tv!

I love to hear from my readers.
Write to me at info@ninjalifehacks.tv or send me mail at:

Mary Nhin
6608 N Western Avenue #1166
Oklahoma City, OK 73116

 @officialninjalifehacks

 @marynhin @officialninjalifehacks
#NinjaLifeHacks

 Mary Nhin   Ninja Life Hacks

 Ninja Life Hacks

Made in the USA
Columbia, SC
23 April 2025

57079153R00020